Stig Hadenius and Birgit Janrup

How they lived in

a Viking Settlement

Translated by Fred Thideman

Illustrated by Ulf Lofgren

Lutterworth Press · Guildford and London

Almost twelve hundred years ago, at the end of the
eighth century A.D., fierce Scandinavian seamen from
the northern lands which are now called Norway, Sweden
and Denmark, came sailing south to raid and plunder
farms, monasteries and settlements on the coasts
and islands of Scotland, Ireland and north-west Europe.
These seamen were called Vikings. Within fifty years
they had reached much further south, to plunder England,
France, Spain, and the coasts of the Mediterranean Sea.
Some of them travelled down the great rivers of Europe into
Germany and Russia; some sailed west across the seas
to discover Iceland, and Greenland, and even the great
continent we now call America. The map on pages 18 and
19 shows some of the Vikings' routes. This book is an
attempt to describe in simple terms what life was like in one of the
Scandinavian settlements from which the Vikings set sail
to trade, to plunder and to explore.

Tua and Vig are eagerly waving
to the Viking ships
which are sailing into the bay.
Their father, their uncle and their three brothers
are on board one of the ships.
They have been away for a long time.
Tua and Vig are looking forward
to seeing them again, and to hearing
about their adventures overseas.

This is the settlement in Scandinavia
where Tua and Vig lived,
about eleven hundred years ago.

At that time much of Scandinavia was covered
by deep forests, and because of this
the Viking settlements were often scattered along the coasts,
between the forests and the sea.
If the people wanted to go
from one village to another,
they had to go by sea, and so
the Viking men quickly became fine sailors.
The Vikings loved and treasured their ships
and gave them long poetical names, such as
Horse of the Gull's Track and *Raven of the Sea*.

The leading ships have almost reached the shore.
As the ships come close to land, there is no longer
enough wind to fill the great sails.
The men lower the sails and
get out the oars instead.

Further out in the bay, there is still enough wind
to drive the other ships forward at a good speed.
Because the wind is blowing towards the shore,
the ships are sailing 'before the wind'.
Viking ships sail fastest and easiest this way.
Tua and Vig think the ships look beautiful.
The men's round shields hang over the sides of the ships,
and the striped sails catch the sunlight.

The Vikings' ships were called 'long ships'.
When you look at pictures of these ships
it is difficult to believe
that they weathered fierce storms and
sailed far across the sea—but they did.
The Vikings were fine shipbuilders
and very good seamen.

Stern

Weather vane

Steering oar

Often, when they built a new ship,
the Vikings would fasten a carved dragon's head at its prow.
Because of this the first long ships were called 'dragons'.
When the Vikings sailed overseas to foreign countries,
and their long ships came thrusting into harbour
or up-river, with the dragon-heads riding high over the water,
they could look very frightening.
At the stern of a long ship, fastened to the right-hand side,
was a massive oar: by turning this oar, the helmsman could
steer the ship. The right-hand side of a ship is still
called 'starboard', and this name comes from the word 'steer':
'steer-board' has gradually turned into 'starboard'.

Prow

Sail

Dragon's head

Oars

We know almost exactly what the long ships looked like,
for three of them were found buried at Oslo in Norway,
and were carefully dug out.
The one which was the best preserved
is called the Oseberg ship.
It was built about eleven hundred years ago,
in the ninth century A.D., and was discovered in 1904.
It is 21 metres long, and is richly carved.

The Oseberg ship

The people who dug up the Oseberg ship discovered that the stern had been turned into a burial chamber.
The woman who was buried there was probably a queen.
Around her in her ship-tomb were a number of treasures.
There were also cooking pots and kitchen utensils,
clothes, food, and jewellery.

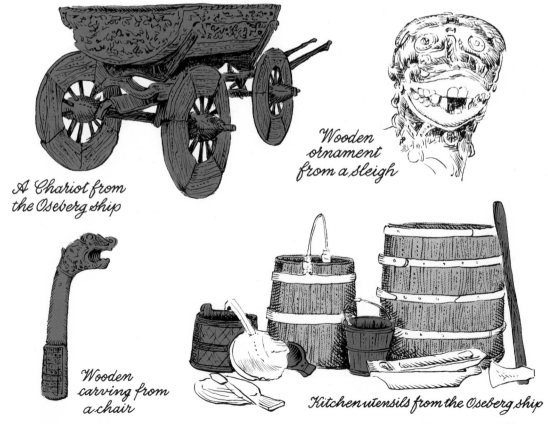

A Chariot from the Oseberg ship

Wooden ornament from a sleigh

Wooden carving from a chair

Kitchen utensils from the Oseberg ship

In the house where Tua and Vig live
there is a feast to celebrate the Vikings' return.
Some of the men are gnawing meat which
has been roasted on a turnspit over the fire.
There is bacon too, and salted fish, and bread.
One of the women is bringing in two horns full of mead,
a drink made with honey.
Now and then someone throws a bone to the dogs.

The women and the children, and the men who are too old
to go to sea any more, are eager to hear
about the Vikings' adventures,
and how they got all the goods they have brought home.
So, when everyone has had enough
to eat and drink,
the Vikings' leader gets ready
to tell the story of their journey.

When they were well out to sea, he says,
there was a terrible storm.
Some of the ships
were so battered by the wind and waves,
that the cargoes were swept away,
and several men were drowned.
When the storm had passed, the ships gathered together again
and the Vikings made fresh plans.
Then the ships whose cargoes were intact sailed on
to sell their goods at a trading town on a big river.

The rest of the Vikings sailed southwards
in search of plunder.
They came to a town at the mouth of a river
and decided it was worth attacking.
They made ready, putting on their helmets,
taking up their shields,
and arming themselves with axes, spears and swords.
Then they went storming up towards the town.
They broke down the gates, killed the defenders,
and plundered the houses.

Meanwhile the other Vikings were making their way
up the river towards the trading town.

In places the river was very shallow,
so shallow that the Vikings could no longer row their ships,
so they had to wade up-river,
pushing the ships through the water.

When they came to a waterfall, they dragged the ships
right up to the top of the cliffs.
Then they rolled each ship along the cliff top
over a row of logs.

In the trading town, merchants were eagerly waiting
to see the Vikings' cargoes of furs and amber.
To get furs to sell, the Vikings simply go hunting
in the northern forests, but to collect the amber
they have to search along the edge of the Baltic Sea.
Sixty million years before the Vikings lived there,
pine trees grew along the Baltic coasts,
and the resin from these ancient trees
has hardened and solidified into shining brownish-gold amber.
The merchants pay the Vikings with bronze or silver,
or, occasionally, with something rare and beautiful,
like a golden bowl or a glass cup.

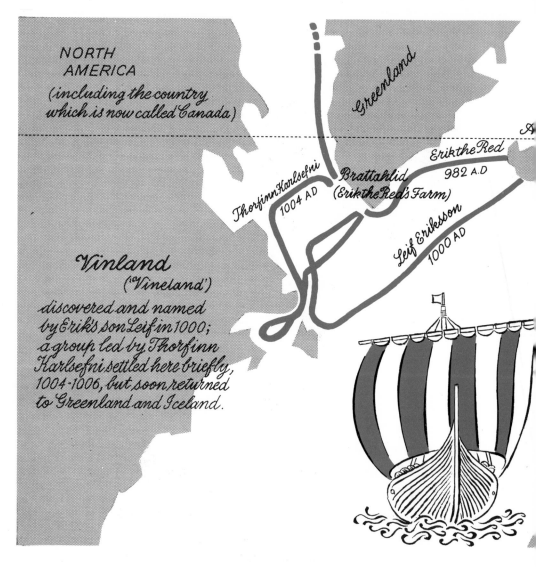

NORTH
AMERICA
*(including the country
which is now called Canada)*

Greenland

A

Thorfinn Karlsefni
1004 AD

*Brattahlid
(Erik the Red's Farm)*

Erik the Red
982 A.D

Leif Eriksson
1000 AD

Vinland
("Vineland")
*discovered and named
by Erik's son Leif in 1000;
a group led by Thorfinn
Karlsefni settled here briefly,
1004-1006, but soon returned
to Greenland and Iceland.*

The red lines on the map show
some of the great journeys the Vikings made.
Leif Eriksson sailed so far west that
he came to the great continent we now call America.
Other Vikings travelled so far south-east, down the rivers
of present-day Russia, that they reached the distant cities
of Baghdad and Istanbul.

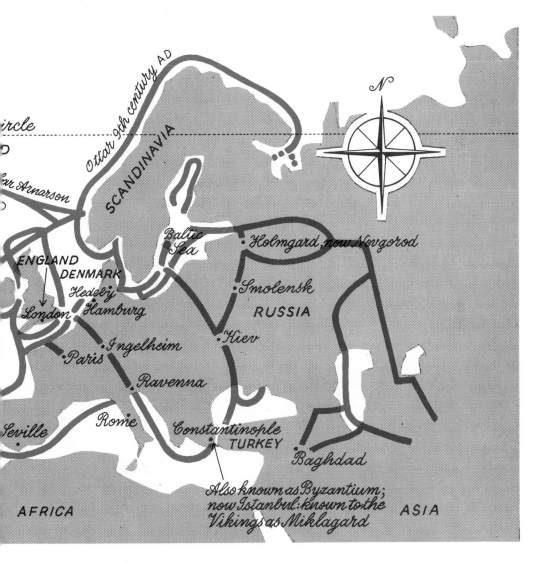

Sometimes the Vikings seized stretches of land overseas
and set up new settlements of their own.
Part of France is still called Normandy because the Normans—
the 'north men'—settled there. There were other settlements
in Russia, England and Friesland.
The Vikings also set up colonies
in two big empty islands: Greenland and Iceland.

Many of the Vikings did not return from their
adventurous journeys.
Some were killed, some captured, some drowned.
When a Viking died overseas, his family
would sometimes set up a stone to his memory.

The stone-worker cut an inscription on the stone.
The inscription gave the dead man's name, and
often it said where he had died.
It was written in letters called runes,
and these memorial stones are now called 'runic stones'.

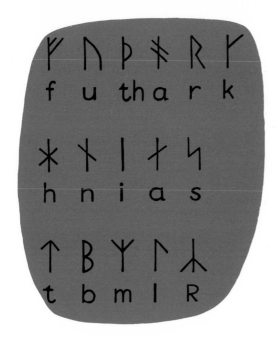

f u tha r k

h n i a s

t b m l R

Modern scholars have learnt how to read Viking runes
and so they have been able to find out a great deal
about the Vikings and their voyages.
Sometimes chronicles and other accounts have survived
from the cities and castles and monasteries
which the Vikings plundered or attacked,
and these help us to find out more.

Sometimes, instead of cutting runes
on the memorial stone,
the stone-worker would cut pictures
and then would colour them.
Pictures like these are very important
for they tell us more about the Vikings.
The stone in the photograph on the left was found
on an island called Gothland, in the Baltic Sea.

When the Vikings reach home
after one of their voyages,
they share out the plunder
and the goods
which they have brought back.
Tua and Vig have been given
a coin each.

Soon the excitement of the Vikings' return is over.
It is time to get on with the farm work.
The Vikings plough the fields,
take care of the animals
and go fishing.
Tua and Vig must do
their share of the work.

There are many other jobs to be done at home.
Here the children's father is making a new bed.
He is a fine carpenter and wood-carver.
Tua and Vig are admiring the tent
which he takes with him on his voyages.

The Vikings like to show off their strength
by competing against one another in various games.
Vig is looking forward to the day
when he will be old enough to join in.
Wrestling is very popular,
and so is a competition
to see which man can lift the heaviest stone.

On the left two Vikings are standing in a loop of rope
and trying to pull one another over,
without using their hands.
Another man is throwing stones at
a wooden marker stuck into the ground.
In winter the Vikings ski and sledge and go skating
on skates made from animal bones.

The Vikings enjoy indoor games too.
Here two of them are playing
by the light of a burning torch.
One of the players sits on the edge
of the long bunk bed.

Tua and Vig are sitting on a fur rug
and trying to play the pipes their father has given them.
Perhaps soon the men will begin to tell stories
of their adventures overseas, and to make plans
for the next voyage.

First published in Great Britain, 1976

Reprinted 1979

Photographs by kind permission of the Statens Historiska Museum

Copyright © 1970 by Stig Hadenius, Birgit Janrup and Ulf Löfgren

Almqvist & Wiksell Förlag AB, Stockholm

English translation copyright © 1976

by Lutterworth Press, Guildford and London

ISBN 0 7188 2199 8

Filmset by Keyspools Limited, Golborne, Lancashire

Printed in Hong Kong